KV-702-440

UNIVERSITY *of* LIMERICK

OLLSCOIL LUIMNIGH

www.ul.ie/library

Gallery Books
Editor Peter Fallon

SELECTED POEMS

Vona Groarke

SELECTED POEMS

Gallery Books

Selected Poems
is first published
simultaneously in paperback
and in a clothbound edition
on 31 March 2016.

The Gallery Press
Loughcrew
Oldcastle
County Meath
Ireland

www.gallerypress.com

*All rights reserved. For permission
to reprint or broadcast these poems,
write to The Gallery Press.*

© Vona Groarke 2016

ISBN 978 1 85235 667 5 *paperback*
    978 1 85235 668 2 *clothbound*

A CIP catalogue record for this book
is available from the British Library.

Selected Poems receives financial assistance
from the Arts Council.

University of Limerick
Library
Supplied in fulfillment of
COPYRIGHT legislation
1600 385 6

the arts council / an chomhairle ealaíon — funding literature — artscouncil.ie

Contents

for Tommy and Eve,
mainstays.

Shale

What leaves us trembling in an empty house
is not the moon, my moon-eyed lover.
Say instead there was no moon
though for nine nights we stood

on the brow of the hill at midnight
and saw nothing that was not
contained in darkness, in the pier light,
our hands, and our lost house.

Small wonder that we tired of this
and chose instead to follow the road
to the back of the island, and broke
into the lighthouse-keeper's house.

We found the lower windows boarded up
and the doors held fast, but one.
Inside we followed the drag of light
through empty rooms of magenta and sky blue.

This house has been decided by the sea.
These rooms are stones washed over by waves
and spray from the lighthouse
by which we undress

to kneel under the skylight.
Our hands and lips are smeared with blackberries.
Your skin, my sloe-skinned lover,
never so sweet, your hand so quiet.

The sea is breaking and unbreaking on the pier.
You and I are making love
in the lighthouse-keeper's house,
my moon-eyed, dark-eyed, fire-eyed lover.

What leaves us trembling in an empty room
is not the swell of darkness in our hands
or the necklace of shale I made for you
that has grown warm between us.

The Riverbed

There is sun in the mirror, my head in the trees.
There is sun in the mirror without me.
I am lying face up on the riverbed.
My lover is swimming above me.

The ribbons he tied in my hair are gone,
gone back to their net in the water.
Instead I have silverweed, speedwell and rue,
where once I had his hands to lie on.

Instead I have silverweed, speedwell and rue,
where once I had his arms beneath me.
His body may come as his body has gone —
and the marl will close over again.

Where are your silverweed, your speedwell now?
They have all gone under the water.
Where is your face in the river now?
Drifting upstream to the moon.

I have walked on the floor of the river with you.
I have walked on the floor of the river.
I would lie on the bed of the river with you.
I will lie on the bed of the river.

Islands

In my house at the edge of the lake
what does not end will not return.
A storm may gather in the stance of trees.
I waited for you. I will sing for you.

When you came to my house for the second time
I had gathered the leaves of the dark in our room.
I lit a fire and a candle to burn
in every window that faced towards your shore.

Won't you call for me at my house by the lake?
Cedar of Lebanon. Silver Birch.
Won't you take me in your boat to the centre of the lake?
Wych elm. Wych elm.

The Tree House

Because someone has been building piles of branches
in the wood I have been remembering your hands.
I propose to make a shelter with a roof and walls of twigs
so the close-knit warp and weft will keep us safe.
I am saying that I want you to return
and will show you how by laying down
a bed of leaves and soft pine cones
where I will kiss you so your body feels the sway.

I want you home. I worry when the wind
is getting up. I'm sure it's only a matter of time
before the ragged pine behind the house
buckles and bears down upon the roof
to splay my body with needles
and sweet-scented cones.

For the Unkept House

Fill the bucket with water.
Fill the coffin with stones.
There's a full moon over the river
and there's no going home.

Make a well in the water.
Make a house in the dark.
There's a full moon over the meadow
and there's no going back.

Sweep the stars from the window.
Sweep the dust from the door.
There's a full moon over the kitchen
and there's no going back anymore.

Break off the branches that withered.
Break off the flowers that grow.
There's a full moon over the gatepost
and there's no place to go.

Pick the stones from the meadow.
Pick the weeds from the grave.
There's a full moon over the threshold
and there's no time to leave.

The Family Photograph

In the window of the drawing room
there is a rush of white as you pass
in which the figure of your husband is,
for a moment, framed. He is watching you.

His father will come, of course,
and, although you had not planned it,
his beard will offset your lace dress,
and always it will seem that you were friends.

All morning you had prepared the house
and now you have stepped out
to make sure that everything
is in its proper place: the railings whitened,

fresh gravel on the avenue, the glasshouse
crystal when you stand in the courtyard
expecting the carriage to arrive at any moment.
You are pleased with the day; all month it has been warm.

They say it will be one of the hottest summers
the world has ever known.
Today your son is one year old.
Later you will try to recall

how he felt in your arms —
the weight of him, the way he turned to you from sleep,
the exact moment when you knew he would cry
and the photograph be lost.

But it is not lost.
You stand, a well-appointed group
with an air of being pleasantly surprised.
You will come to love this photograph

and will remember how, when he had finished,
you invited the photographer inside
and how, in celebration of the day,
you drank a toast to him, and summertime.

Rain Bearers

When the others have gone we row out to the island.
A darkness clots the skyline to the west.
There's been talk that summer will not last.

We stand against the trees for an hour or more
waiting for the evening to dissolve in lake water
and music from an endless barbeque.

The seagulls snag on the water.
The line you trace from them across the lake
ends in a beat of pebbles skimmed against the shore.

The fire in the car park eventually collapses.
By midnight they are packing up for home.
We watch until the last tail light

stutters behind the woods and fades away.
You shout out our names to claim possession.
The silence brings a sense of being adrift.

In this first home we sit together
calling out the colours of the clouds
as amber, pitch or amethyst.

We cup our hands around them,
passing them between us like small gifts.
You say if anything is easy it is this.

That seems enough. When I close my eyes
there are shadows where the shapes of cloud began.
Your hand, when you lean to touch me, smells of rain.

Indoors

It breaks apart as water will not do
when I pull, hard, away from me,
the corners bunched in my two hands
to steer a true and regulated course.

I plunge the needle through and through,
dipping, tacking, coming up again.
The ripple of thread that follows pins,
out of its depth, a shallow hem.

I smooth the waves and calm the folds.
Then, to ensure an even flow,
I cast a line which runs from hook to hook
and pulls the net in overlapping pleats.

Which brings me to the point where I am
hanging a lake, by one shore, in my room,
to swell and billow between the light
and opaque, unruffled dark.

I step in. The room closes round me
and scarcely puckers when I move my limbs.
I step out. The path is darkened where I walk,
my shadow steaming off in all this sun.

Folderol

I have been walking by the harbour
where I see it's recently sprayed
that *Fred loves Freda*, and *Freda cops Fred*.
Which reminds me of you, and the twenty-four

words for 'nonsense' I wrote on your thighs and back
with passion-fruit lipstick and mascara pens
the night you came home from her house with some cock-
and-bull story of missed connections and loose ends.

Including, for the record: blather, drivel, trash,
prattle, palaver, waffle, balderdash, gibberish, shit.
Thinking I had made a point of sorts, but not
so sure when I woke up to find my own flesh

covered with your smudged disgrace
while you, of course, had vanished without trace.

The Lighthouse

I heard her tell the story another way.
She set it, not in the village, where
the parish priest was telling the crowd
about light in the darkness
and the dawn of a new age —

she set it in the kitchen of their house,
with three women resting
and the day's work done. She told it
so we would listen for the music
of the room when it was still:

the rustle of the fire in the grate;
the single held note of a teaspoon
from which the knitting needles took their cue;
the steady flutter of the carriage clock
that kept their breath in check.

One of them might sleep and her nodding glasses
snag the firelight and scatter it
around the room to return in the more
familiar shine of cups on the dresser,
copper pans, her sister's wedding band.

In the village, a crowd of overcoated men
sent up a cheer for progress and prosperity
for all . . .
                And in the length of time
it took to turn a switch and to make light
of their house, three women saw themselves

stranded in a room that was nothing like
their own, with pockmarked walls

and ceiling stains, its cobwebs and its grime:
their house undone and silenced
by the clamour of new light.

The Empty House

When we are gone the house will close over us
as though we'd been swimmers in an unmoved sea.
The cisterns will unruffle, the fridge will wheeze on,
and the shape we made in the bed will pucker out.

The house will replace us with sounds of its own:
the shuffle of pages as we pull the door hard,
the phone ringing out, the occasional clock,
and only the letterbox will break the settled air.

All these shadows from the beech tree in the back
that close on my arm as I reach to turn the key
will swell with a glitter that will take in the room
and, this evening, drain what is left of us away.

Other People's Houses

for Conor

Last night I walked to a house where we
once lived. It's not looking good.
There's been a fire and the roof's caved in.
The garden's scotched with grass and weeds
and most of the windows are through.

The ceiling of the sitting room is upended
on the floor. No trace now of the yellow
couch that was our 'amour prop',
or the stack of romantic novels you had me
stand up on to save your aching back.

Or the radio we lived by in those days,
you with your cricket and creaky plays
on the BBC; me with my news on the
hour, every hour, lest something
outside of us should ever change.

Or the soggy mattress where we sailed
beyond the beyonds and, somehow,
back again to wake each morning
to the blue of our eyes and the three
mile trek for newspapers and milk.

Or the porch where I used to write those
flowery poems before I knew you so well,
halfway between the In- and Outdoors,
where one time, looking two ways at once,
I saw you stranded in both, and thought

I would throw in my lot with yours.
Which is about it. We lived in
other people's houses then. Now,
we have a stake in a place of our own
which keeps us steady and tied.

I want you to know, not that nothing
is lost — even I could not promise
so much — but that something remains,
here, even after so many years:
the starlings are still nesting in the eaves.

And last night as I watched them
their circular orbit put me in mind
of the rhumba you danced with a bumblebee
right there at the gate, on the day that we left
this house behind us, together and for good.

Outdoors

It happens so easily. We've been watching trees
gather shadow on the wall, on the lookout
for a moment when we might call it a day
and settle for the night. But only our room
is losing ground, while nothing outside is lost.

In the time it takes for him to turn to meet my eye
we have missed it; it has happened without us again.
I give in, put on the light, and watch for him to be
stranded, confronting me from the garden, his back
to me in the kitchen, his eyes, in the glass, on me.

What does it matter that we have made a home
where we can draw the curtains and talk of tomorrow,
if we are thinking of this: the shapes we made in darkness,
our kitchen at sea on the lawn, our table set out
in the branches, our faces marooned in stars?

The Verb 'to herringbone'

Something beginning with slightness
and possibly taken from there.
As though unheard of, inauspicious,
the way a pheasant or a wood pigeon
will find a point of no return, on a lorryless
side-road or on the lee side of an air.
Something begun and veering off at once

as though to double back would be the point of it
and diminution would be a slight recall:
something with an underscore,
though currently unsure how to proceed
or to convince. Like the verb 'to herringbone'
or the air displaced by flight.

Flight

Effortless and uninscribed, the sky
has earthed everything outside
where even bleached flight-lines

are ground as small as the pellucid breastbone
of a golden oriole or wren
between the thumb and palm of my right hand

to a powder that settles on this:
the point at which two rumours coalesce,
one to do with vision, one with voice.

One minute, it's ruse and colour,
the next, wingspan and whir.
And who's to say just what occurs

when something loses the run
of itself and slips airborne
and downwind into the auburn

undertone of flight. And so, away
from the calligraphy of swallows
on a page of cloud; tern prints on snow

that almost lead somewhere,
but then break off and stutter
underground, or into breathless air.

Closer to hand there is the slight
precision of the black and white
and its close score and countercut

that becomes what happens here,
between these squat characters
and a thinning fiction keen to aspire

to a sequence of hard words laid
one on the other and back again
like a schoolgirl's braid,

chaotic and restrained; that cannot
be taken in hand; that's here now, but
working up to clearing itself out;

soon to be thin air; nothing to write
home about; an advancing quiet
that throws this into shadow underneath

where, by way of leavetaking this time,
death, like a moth in a paper lantern,
is rattling in even these lines.

The Way It Goes

Choose one version. Turn it. Let it go. See how it spins,
what it fastens, what it sheds. You could call it a thread
that leads you or a tie that binds, but this is a landscape
wasted by the fervour of clean lines. You were one
for happenstance and the story that belied its ordained end.
And where in all that tangle of fresh starts and dead stops
could I find a place where I might rightfully begin?

Side-lit corridors, six-panelled doors, copper pans
and ancestors in rows like chimney stacks and poplar trees
that hide a nest of cottages laid in grass that grows too tall
and is strewn with pig-tailed daughters and knock-kneed sons
who face the world with a different, sidelong view
in which the furrows and fencing posts head one way,
and the ditches and the open road another.

The wall of the yard is darned with stones from the house.
Someone says there was a family of them, though what
became of them is no-man's guess. Now and then, something
turns up: a horseshoe or the base of a crockery pot. And once,
a slate with a fretwork of lines that may have been a name
or half a name — Fox or Cox, maybe. A hard sound to finish with,
for certain, though the start of it is something we can't say.

There must have been other houses that fell in on themselves
this way. I think of you and your inside-out voice going over
and over a brittle, third-hand past. That was towards the end.
'There was no one in the corridors, the windows were shut up.'
And later, dragged outside by the scruff of another incident,
how they walked and passed no one but the remaining
animals which did not avert their eyes. How many roads now?

How many eyes? In those days nothing came of anything,
the wind whipped their heels and words, it was every man
for himself and the billycans' rattling made herds of them.
And night no mercy either, dropping past the point
where breath was cupped and handed round, where
there was nothing but a steady count that took you
to dawn's luckless hour and stories of another night survived.

April. An excess of lilac turned them round towards home. May
brought rhubarb so their breath soured over intermittent fire.
June. A memory, their mouths were stopped with it. Then
the summer fruits came in, and nothing for it but sweetness,
an aftertaste of briar. When the boy died they couldn't bury him
but left him ashen with soil and recompense, though
his mouth and fingers were smeared with a likeness of blood.

You favoured stories that end in silent death and someone
obvious to blame. You left me your grandmother's ruby ring
and the tune of a song she used to sing. We cleared your house
before the sale (it barely filled a skip), and I took cuttings
from the garden that have never really thrived. So it goes.
My sister got the furniture. With my share I bought a plot
by the sea where I grow poppies and cornflowers and weeds.

I lived with them, though it was never mine, unless you count
the tree he gave me, or the stones I lodged in the wall. Once
you picked an egg up from the grass to say it was the same blue
as his eyes. Enough. The flags are yellow, the rushes green,
the years have made them grow. I threw soil from their grave
on the rosebush by the door. It yields a good and heavy scent
which you would say is dark and rank and given to excess.

I have known the give of fruit with its too-easy flow.
I have walked those roads. If I can double back to my hearth,
my bed and my intentions, I mean it as no ordinary return.
What can I say? I wake to a taste of dreams I don't recognize.
I call your name. Or I follow the path of dog roses
and wayfarer's friend that are always here, that pay me no heed,
or that bend as I pass, and straighten as soon as I'm gone.

Maize

for Tommy

The Faber Castells ripen in your hand.
You've been drawing since breakfast:
sky after sky, face after face, but something
in yours says they're not quite right.

Every fresh character is dipped
in your range of skins —
beige, primrose, lemon, sand —
and still found wanting.

You finally settle on maize
but not before almost a sheaf
of paper has been scorched
with a repertoire of possible flesh.

The pages rustle into place. I'm watching you
and every irreproachable, off-tone face
is your own in the back of our first white Polo
when summer landed you wide-eyed at the door.

Your head then was marooned in arrival
like our papier-mâché moon.
See how you've given it petals,
wings, hair I can run my hand through

the way the wind cross-hatches
an open field where corn is sweetening
in its cornsilk skin; where yellow
falters, gold begins to maize.

Tonight of Yesterday

for Eve

The evening slips you into it, has kept a place for you
and those wildwood limbs that have already settled on
the morning. The words you have for it are flyblown now
as the dandelion you'll whistle tomorrow into a lighter air.
But, tonight, your sleep will be as round as your mouth,
berried with the story of sunlight finally run to ground.
You are all about tomorrow. The moon has your name
memorized: the curl of your back; your face, an open book.

Family

My mother has gone and bought herself a piglet
because none of us comes to visit anymore.
George has good manners and is clean in his ways:
he is courtly, thoughtful, easy to amuse.
He goes to Mass with her, and sits sweetly
while she trots up to receive. He doesn't stray.
She has made a cot for him in the kitchen
where he turns in on our old clothes cut to size.

One Sunday I call on the way to somewhere else.
She props him up beside me in the high chair
and he fixes me with those dreary dark blue eyes.
When I tell him I'm glad he's there when I can't be,
he answers 'thank you' in a voice too like my own,
then bids me sit and make myself at home.

Veneer

Give me my hand on his neck and his back to my breast,
my heart ruffling his ribs and their flighty charge.
Give me the seagrass bristles on his shoulder blades
and his spine, courteous and pliable to my wrist.

His back is a child's drawing of seagulls flocked.
I knuckle the air undone by their windward flight
and draw from their dip and rise my linear breath.

Were he standing, my tongue could graze the whorl
at the base of his neck and leave my hand to plane
the small of his close-grained waist.

Were he lying down, I'd crook in the hollow
of him and, with my index finger, slub the mole
at the breech of his back that rounds on darkness
like a knot in veneer: shallow, intricate, opaque.

Cuttings

Today the outing is to Castle Proud, and we are taking the bus.
Sheila saw it in the paper. It was her idea.
Her grandmother used to work for the Prouds
as a scullery maid for seven years and, never once,

in all that time, she said, did they call her by her real name.
I said they must have called her something
and Sheila said they called her Rosie, because Cook said
that suited her so much better than Pauline.

Sheila's granny told her that Castle Proud
had the nicest flowers of anywhere she'd worked.
The avenues were thick with jasmine
and the lawn had camomile and mint in it that were

invisible but, when you walked over the grass,
the scent your feet released was something else.
We're for the half-ten tour and, afterwards,
we want to walk those gardens and the lawns.

We have canvas holdalls in our shoulder bags
and a pair of secateurs. We're gardeners, you see,
Sheila and me. We swop clippings and advice.
We're martyrs to the programmes on TV.

When we get back we'll have a whole new crop
of cuttings to take root amongst our dahlias and phlox.
I'm hoping for gardenias and, maybe, fleur-de-lis.
They're quite exotic. You don't get them round here.

Imperial Measure

'We have plenty of the best food, all the meals being as good as if
served in a hotel. The dining-room here is very comfortable.'
   — P H Pearse, the GPO, Easter 1916, in a letter to his mother

The kitchens of the Metropole and Imperial hotels yielded
   up to the Irish Republic
their armory of fillet, brisket, flank. Though destined for
   more palatable tongues,
it was pressed to service in an Irish stew and served on fine
   bone china
with bread that turned to powder in their mouths. Brioche,
   artichokes, tomatoes
tasted for the first time: staunch and sweet on Monday but,
   by Thursday,
they had overstretched to spill their livid plenitude on the
   fires of Sackville Street.

A cow and her two calves were commandeered. One calf was
   killed,
its harnessed blood clotting the morning like news that
   wasn't welcome
when, eventually, it came. The women managed the blood
   into black puddings
washed down with milk from the cow in the yard who smelt
   smoke on the wind
and fire on the skin of her calf. Whose fear they took for loss
   and fretted with her
until daylight crept between crossfire and the sights of
   Marrowbone Lane.

Brownies, Simnel cake, biscuits slumped under royal icing.
   Éclairs with their cream
already turned. Crackers, tonnes of them: the floor of
   Jacobs' studded with crumbs,

39

so every footfall was a recoil from a gunshot across town,
  and the flakes
a constant needling in mouths already seared by the one
  drink — a gross
or two of cooking chocolate, stewed and taken without
  sweetener or milk.
Its skin was riven every time the ladle dipped but, just as
  quickly, it seized up again.

Nellie Gifford magicked oatmeal and a half-crowned loaf to
  make porridge
in a grate in the College of Surgeons where drawings of field
  surgery
had spilled from Ypres to drench in wounds the whitewashed
  walls
of the lecture hall. When the porridge gave out, there was
  rice:
a biscuit tin of it for fourteen men, a ladleful each that
  scarcely knocked
the corners off their undiminished appetites; their vast,
  undaunted thirst.

The sacks of flour ballasting the garrison gave up their
  downy protest under fire.
It might have been a fall of Easter snow sent to muffle the
  rifles or to deaden the aim.
Every blow was a flurry that thickened the air of Boland's
  Mill, so breath
was ghosted by its own white consequence. The men's
  clothes were talced with it,
as though they were newborns, palmed and swathed, their
  foreheads kissed,
their grips unclenched, their fists and arms first blessed and,
  then, made much of.

The cellars of the Four Courts were intact at the surrender,
  but the hock
had been agitated, the Reisling set astir. For years the wines
  were sullied
with a leaden aftertaste, although the champagne had as full
  a throat as ever,
and the spirits kept their heady confidence, for all the stock-
  piled bottles
had chimed with every hit, and the calculating scales above
  it all
had had the measure of nothing, or nothing if not smoke,
  and then wildfire.

Ghosts

Not exactly. Something like breath on your cheek
or an aftertaste of summer, years ago; one,
two metallic notes with the cadence of a name;
silverfish throwing your reflection off a beat.
Or a peony petal blown onto your path.

I don't think so. The children know.
They breathe ghosts into January
that stand for the split second it takes
to take us in, and then they're off
as though released, like figments of the air.

Windmill Hymns

In the shadow of the windmill we put down our lives.
Something about its girth and ballast, the sun on its back,
its shiftless, amber absolute foreclosed on other options.
We put down our lives as if for a moment — a break for tea
or to deal with an enquiry in the yard — and something about

its dereliction shut down at once on the chance of things
ever picking up again. Now, seven years on, this is us
finding the storeys equal to our time and too ornamental.
Even its decay does not refuse the compliment of sunshine,
the way the moon rubs up against it, or clouds distract

themselves upon its brim. What we were after was a stopgap
for the lives we thought we'd live, that wouldn't be banked
in small talk, disappointments, lack of cash; the intended,
blue-sky lives that would have us tilting at an evening do,
with arms like French film stars and mouthfuls of moonlight

to slip us downstream into bed. That was then. I lie. It never was.
This instead is the relief of getting nowhere, of knowing
from the start how it must end. The same momentum,
selfsame pace that drags itself and all its consequence
over the bones of another rattled year. I suppose, at some point,

it will stop, and all the shunt and grind of the day-to-day
come creaking towards another new conclusion, a new plan:
the last sacks loaded, the carts dismissed, handshakes,
gates pulled shut from the outside and then a silence
gaining on the sails, settling there, the way birds do, the air,

the damp, the mould will all do now. How long before the wood
lets itself down on willowherb at bay in shuttered light;
before doors give up the ghost; floors shrug the way windows
cannot bring themselves to do, until local lads with slingshots
and deadeyes see to them? How long until the weeds take hold

and starlings, like quicksilver, like silverfish, like a fastness
of silver spilled out on the stones? And us? We don't move.
Our way of holding on, of saying, 'We've stayed too long',
is like the way the children have of stopping play
to stand stock-still under the whir of starlings' hide-and-seek.

That what's missing should be called 'the coping' makes me
want to lay my face against the stone; let ivy root in my teeth;
weather grout my skin, my eyes take on the evening and its down.
Let my children stand within an inch of my life, so the way
their breath aspires could be the sky, or something close, to me.

To Smithereens

You'll need a tiller's hand to steer this through
the backward drift that brings you to, as always,
one fine day. August 1979. A sunlit Spiddal beach.

Children ruffle the shoreline. Their nets are full
of a marvellous haul of foam and iridescent sand
and water that laughs at them as it wriggles free.

They hardly care: they are busy spilling buckets
of gold all over the afternoon. But further back
something spreads over the beach like scarlet dye

on the white-hot voice of the radio. The mams
and aunts pinned onto Foxford rugs put down
their scandalous magazines and vast, plaid flasks

as a swell from over the rocks showers them
with words like rowboat, fishing, smithereens.
You hear it too, the news that falls in slanted beats

like metal shavings sprayed from a single,
incandescent point to dispel themselves
as the future tense of what they fall upon.

Let's say you are lifted clear of the high-tide line
into another order of silence. Exchange the year.
The cinema's almost empty. She has taken you

to *Gandhi* at the Ritz. You are only a modernist
western wall away from the Shannon and the slipknot
of darkness the river ties and unties in the scenes.

Her breath is caught up in it: she's nodding off.
Her head falls back on the crimson plush and then
her carriage bears her on and on, shunting towards

the very point where all the journeys terminate
with the slump and flutter of an outboard engine
reddening the water with its freight. It's here

that every single thing casts off, or is brightly cast,
into a flyblown, speckled plural that scatters tracks
in the heat and dust of the locked projection room.

The railway bridge one up from ours shakes out
each of its iron rails in readiness, and she is woken
by words that spill over the confluence of the Ganges

and the Shannon at our backs. 'To smithereens?',
she says. 'I'm pretty sure it's Indian. It means
to open (like an Albertine); to flower.'

The Local Accent

This river is pronounced by granite drag.
It is a matter of inflection, of knowing what
to emphasize, and what to let drift away,
just as a slipping aspen leaf makes barely a flicker,
one gaffe in the conversation between the current
and the flow; a stifled yawn, a darkness reimbursed;

while, underneath, the thing that falls through shadow
is full of its own occasion. Weighty and dull,
it longs for water, the lacquer and slip of it,
the way it won't allow for brightness on its back,
but flips around to where its fall is a wet-wool,
sodden thing about to break at any moment, and undo.

Something is coming loose like aspen leaves, or froth.
Or maunder, letting itself down like rain into a river
immersed in getting on with what it separates:
the sulk of damp soil; the stiff articulation of the shore,
the giddy vowels sprayed over the drag and ebb
of voices leaking through the rain over the town.

Everything arrives at a standstill under the bridge.
The town grips the river and all the words for elsewhere
or for being there have had their edges worn off
and their meanings powdered to a consonantal darkness
where they dissolve, like happenings, into traffic
and asphalt, or otherwise, in the river and its silt.

This river is pitched so far from the sea
it announces itself in elision, as though everything
unsaid could still bed down in depth and unison,
underwriting words for going on and every other way
in and out of this one place. Excepting the blood-red
trickle of sky, and what it overrides, what slips beneath.

Athlones

A town racked on a river, too far in,
too cosseted by land to be tossed
and turned by anything so flighty as a sea.

Always under the governess eye of Lough Ree,
bearing down in mourning silks
with a sudden tetchiness on boats

that splutter their poorly learned past tenses
much too late. The same boats on the river
are like firstborns in a county family

propped up on surnames and wide berths
on a current lately civilized, its face
scrubbed clean and all its trawl

of Latin verbs and parlour songs
boxed clean away for tomorrow morning's
class. This is a river taken in hand

and made to march along the fastness
of the Castle and the Barracks wall: it keeps
the swell of Connaught well at bay.

A two-faced river, holding the line between
the Pale and Irishtown, the to-and-fro of siege
or confiscation, dual strategies of granite and edict.

A river kept in check, though dampness
slakes the rights and wrongs, the black
and white of its unequal board

where all the lines cast themselves off
to be submerged in what cannot keep quiet,
or in tow. All its words have been vouchsafed

in the low-slung building opposite the church
that put its toe in the water once and froze,
eye to eye with upper decks and punters

waving in at readers picking past the watermark
for a change of plot or a first edition
of the way things ought to be.

Its marbled covers might anticipate a sunlight
that could open out a river's darknesses
as onyx slips or deckled, gold-leaf pages.

The apartment windows jostle for its preference
like dancers primmed in shoes too small,
their candied thank yous quite sucked dry

and their bouquet of responses clasped too close.
Such light as ventures in their recess
advances in shifts of obligation and poor grace,

stammers a thin compliment and is lured away
by a river just then letting fall a beaded string
of laughter on a wildly polished floor.

The same light tinkles down through Northgate Street
like someone running late, all streaming hair
and necklaces that chink like moorings

in a breeze, only to trip on the butcher's awnings
or be splayed in Burgess' window like a pomegranate
on an oilcloth, spilling out some exotic largesse.

It roots then in the florist's bins for cellophane
to dabble in, for colour to be sweet-talked
into giving its metallic sheath the slip.

The child with the stick of rock knows how it goes:
he is holding up the wrapper so it crinkles into rainbows
on his palm. In the Genoa Café the girl manoeuvring

her Coke like a hand-mirror to snare the arc of brilliance
on the cloth knows too. So does the man angling a suitcase
to entice a thread of it from the swags of a plastic raincoat

coming through. A car goes past him once,
its fender spilling a hoard of light on the asphalt
and his shoe. Or the wrist that is opening a window

on the second floor clips the sun with the face of a watch,
and sprays shavings of it down on the highlights of a head
just then emerging from Estelle's Salon. Or the woman

with her bag of books turning her head to check for cars
so her glasses flick a shimmer from the river
over the bulkhead shadow of St Peter's and St Paul's.

Or the sparkler on another woman's hand
slewing announcements all over town, with
a rumour of charm in every unmatched word.

Like the saffron accent of awnings
on Indian stalls in Market Square
leaning into a clatter of hangers

that fills the seams of dresses that were
too much even when the Ritz stood still,
décolleté and shoulder-hunched,

with a hemline skirting the river
like a cotton thread spun out
between Calcutta and Hollywood;

between a full-frontal prairie sunset
and a midland dawn; between two
provinces and two elective ends.

The Galway train declaims
the middle ground, cleaves the river
to an agitated squall, and takes

hardly more than a minute to cross
the bridge, shake out its wingtip
carriages and take off again

to another place that is a fraction closer
to something about to happen
or to conclude a sweet arrangement with

a reason to go on or to go under
at the point where more than accent
slips between at one and alone,

washing up against the urge to be,
at last, at home, pacing over paths
that cast off as I do, in a bed of words,

loose as years ago, and coursing still.
That could, at any second, come
asunder in a darkening hour, or gather

as pleats of rain into a pleated river.
What matter? Its end will still engage
with gold and promises, and nothing

about the gunmetal sheen of the pavement
or the flurry of people with one purpose
in their minds can alter that. So let blinds

be drawn, cars spill muck and piecemeal darkness
on his shoes. Let the woman step out of Estelle's,
uncurl her umbrella, then head off; let the flowers

contract, the pomegranate wither,
the conversation in the Genoa pick up
in the half-light of confidences almost spilled,

a gleam of observations over tea. Let readers
borrow their new order of words: stood in the door
of Fr Mathew Hall, they are sentries waiting

for the castle to brighten, for the church to lift
its veil of winter, for their cars to be no longer
lost to them in the swell of Market Square.

Let jackdaws overawe the bastion,
gulls pierce the Shannon's tireless drone,
traffic pick up from the lights and carry on.

Let computers wind down, office doors
conduct their two-step to the tune of what falls
between See you tomorrow and Oh, by the way . . .

Step out a while. Those footfalls could be stitches
in an overcoated dusk. The river soars alongside;
evening attends. The wind chimes in the Gallery

set aside their rufflings for the night. The final note
of their cadenza could be the first in the waltz
that plays over and over in the Royal Hotel

as the calendar clicks into place and all the clocks
keep time. The sound of them is like smithereens
of coloured glass; a smattering of rain on the ash trees

of Accommodation Road; like the tinkle of light
on a river learned by rote, if not by heart. The sky
concedes. Any minute now will come release.

Call Waiting

Three times I call, three times you're engaged.
You know I am incoming, according to the voice:
my call heralds itself with two round pips,
beads on a chain of intimate, dead air
coiled like the flex around your index finger now
as you stand in the kitchen of the house where I am not
and where, upstairs, is the ring he gave her,
that she gave to me and his dovetailed dress-jacket
she begged me not to wear but I did anyway,
sixteen, blue-haired, all my plans laid out as parallels
marked with a ruler and measured for space
claimed as gracelessly as those black squares
we inked on our fingernails. I must have been nine
when I learned to split a circle three-ways
from just above the centre out, like the Pye sign
in the country town we drove through yesterday.
The boy who told my fortune in Greece
said I had too many lines: they threw him
every which way and he couldn't tell my heart
from head or how the life would span,
but he was right about the indoor garden
I planted with ivy and the little gate that opens
on nothing but its own three arduous notes.
There's a leaf of copper beech in my hand now
and the voice is telling me to hold for a connection.
I tear along the veins and find I am left
with one trefoil that splays like any fish spine
or the crow's feet that have settled round my eyes.
My call is brushing up against yours now
like a ten-cent coin between two fifties in my pocket
or a marble with three colours curled
to skim the arc of two others in its path.
Or like the way your breath on the back of my hand
had three things to say, and none of them got said.

The Game of Tennis in Irish History

Blame Lady Alice Howard and her diary of 1873
patrolling the white line around the one green space
at Shelton Abbey where the Parnells, Charlie and Fanny,

banter in and back, skirting the net, filling the hours
between politics and tea. She looks up: a weak breeze riffles
the pages on which she has pinned the afternoon

in Indian ink, and their laughter scatters in choked aspen trees
where sunlight, regardless, upends both the game
and the ambitions of those plainly put-down words.

Another volume: Spring 1921. The diary laments
they have had a blow: a permit for the motor was refused.
Not so in Ballyturin House where the tennis party

has broken up in salvered tea and calls for a reprise.
Which might itself have been an entry from the diary,
save for the culminating flourish of bodies, one slumped

over the bonnet like an umpire checking the chalk for dust
or the volley of shots like a flurry of late calls, or the opening
account of play stalled on the lodge gates oddly closed.

After that, it's a holding game, put down to delivery,
service skills, to foot faults or to where advantage falls
and to how often the metaphor is required to work the line

between incident and outrage, between the ins and outs
of the intent or outcome, to the calling out or not in
or only just, to the over and eventual out, out, out.

Bournemouth

Jane of the vanilla skin and me
in the linen room of the Cumberland Hotel
just killing time. She cut my hair.
Or maybe I cut hers. Something, anyway.
We'd pink uniforms, short nails,
jokes about used condoms.
She sang Blondie songs like they were news,
wore blue eyeliner and did extra rooms.
We took a trip to Bournemouth
and ate ice cream with our sandals kicked to shore.
She said, 'Nobody talks of leaving anymore.'
Then it was August. We both went home.

Juniper Street

We go to sleep by artificial moonlight.
The floodlit stadium times itself out at midnight
and a thicker weave of darkness plies the room.

We sleep under the eaves where nights of late
have eddied in the wind's plump, elevated arch.
We wake to only dawn's blindsided glaze.

Just last week the icicle tree at our door
was in full bloom. The breeze made a show of it.
We picked one bud with the longest stem

to set in the freezer where it has since drooped,
given itself up to the kitchen's heated breath.
Now March is opening and closing, like a valve.

Snow-melt in the gutters keeps new time,
ice slurs on the lean-to, the Swiss Alps
of the swimming pool drape over our own roof line

and the ticking flagpole sees out the month with us.
This morning the trash was dappled on the lawn
where squirrels are sifting with Victorian aplomb,

tails aloft like pinkies off a cup. Chrome riplets from
next door's chimes, like first notes of some oriole
or wren, slip over the path, are pounced on by a hawk

in the gingko preening himself to call upon a light
just come into its own. Then the laburnum school bus
swerves into view, and the children's on-the-run

goodbyes settle on the porch with my unplanted kiss.
I am queen of the morning: nothing to do but to fiddle
words or quote the gilt-edge of our neighbour's forsythia

gaining on our own trim laurel shrub. Or tell you now
that even in January, with our snow boots lined up
in the hall, I slipped your leather glove onto my hand

and felt the heat of you as something on the turn
that would carry us over the tip of all that darkness
and land us on the stoop of this whole new world.

Some Weather

Among the things
(though these are not things)
I did to pre-empt the storm were:
upturn, stow, disconnect,
shut down, shutter, shut.

But, while the house sulked,
the sky scolded
and I observed an hour's breadth,
the storm tossed out its tinsmith verbs
somewhat to the west.

Away

We have our own smallholding:
persimmon tree, crawl space, stoop,
red earth basement, ceiling fans, a job.

Hours I'm not sure where I am,
flitting through every amber
between Gales and Drumcliffe Road.

I paint woodwork the exact azure
of a wave's flipside
out the back of Spiddal pier

and any given morning pins
a swatch of sunlight
to my purple shamrock plant.

My faithless heart ratchets
in time to slower vowels,
higher daylight hours.

I grow quiet. Yesterday
I answered in a class of Irish
at the checkout of Walgreen's.

I walk through the day-to-day
as if ferrying a pint glass
filled to the brim with water

that spills into my own accent:
pewtered, dim, far-reaching,
lost for words.

An American Jay

Midterm, and the kids hang round like wisps of summer,
spinning channels between the election and Iraq,
laughing only at ads for the new Hummer

dealership on Silas or Larry Cobalt's Rent-a-Wreck
or the pre-Thanksgiving clear-out at K-Mart.
Even the radio doubts the space between a rock

and a hard place on the war front. It launches in on Marx
which is round about the point where I switch, finally,
to an Anglophile mid-morning with the Kumars

or *All Creatures Great and Small* or *The Royle Family*
or any other one of a hundred ways to fritter
a tea-break or two on what's billed, not funnily

enough, as Classic Hour. But not even the future
tense of wheatfields in Ohio or plain-speak in Kansas
can pull us away from a pre-paid, half-hour feature

on William Carlos Williams reading 'Queen Anne's
Lace', a recording that sheds decades and darkness
as ripe as this Fall's haws or quinces

left to rot on the ground for lack of a crew to harvest
even this sound bite. Two experts pull rank (or
what you will) on this morning's conversational largesse.

They're at it hammer and tongs, spite and rancour
name-calling, the works. I turn off, compose
myself in the back bedroom for the crankier

exercise of the afternoon's hour on campus
during which I'll try to praise and encourage
my nine students to find some new compass

that points beyond the fashionable entourage
of sentimental dudes and soulful sidekicks
who plan on moving, after May, to Anchorage

to finish novels, waitress, work as psychics
in the packed-ice atmosphere of a northern funfair
with its stoical rides and half-hearted high jinks.

But for now they're stuck with my unfair
insistence on their coming up with a ballad
of sorts for next Tuesday. I give good build-up, fanfare

and blow, Keats and Goldsmith, the full absurd ballet
of merciless broads, mad dogs and Englishmen, all equally
metered, fastened to a narrative of this week's ballot

or a news report of something local: spinach and e-coli,
Jerry Swaim, plucked from his job in a Raleigh abattoir,
to serenade the First Lady with Rat Pack classics on his ukulele.

I hand out clippings. A check-out girl in CVS is an avatar.
A preacher is arrested for an international drugs deal.
The Warthogs ballpark is declared too amateur.

Sue Zeller advises strongly against Drink and Dial.
Op-eds address the Presidential lack of hard headlines.
Nimrod's has a lunchtime special on tikka and dhal.

My students smirk. I'm square. Fixed in the headlights
of form and tradition, I tell them, 'Next, it's an ode'.
The news is welcomed like a bad dose of head lice.

I remind Sally about the sonnet I'm still owed.
She smiles, says she'll get to it after her midterm on *Hamlet*.
I'm not sure if she thinks I'm quaint or just plain odd.

I treat myself to Sancerre with my omelette.
It's been a tough day and I still have a thesis on Nelly Sachs
by a student who evidently hasn't heard of an umlaut

to get through. Bill Clinton's on TV, playing sax.
When I come to, a biopic of Tiger or Vijay
seems like the loneliest possible alternative to sex.

I'm too old for this. I feel like some hoary, washed-up hoojah
on the edge of that funfair, waiting for the carousel
to jolt into life like a wound-up hummingbird or jay

to circulate a sincere song of desire, blaze, arousal.

Horses

The drier gives the first two notes
of 'In the Bleak Midwinter'
before giving up the ghost.

The clothes horse will have to come
into its own, propped in the bath
like a newborn foal, all joints and poise,

as if sizing up the hurdle of the one blue rim
that stands before our backyard fence
and the thin-lipped creek

that skirts two fields below a road
I knew the ins and outs of when
he used to unpick his day, step by step,

flat cap and hip flask, whistling
an ascending scale that tilted,
over the top, into the ditch.

He bred horses, fenced them in clean lines,
swaddled them in cast-off woollens,
gave them our names,

walked out to stand with them
one Christmas Day; brought back
to the house a voice infused

with inland fields and breath
that flocked above them
like damp flannel, streaming silks.

Aubade

You say that you heard piano chords rustling in the night;
that you woke once and saw me there, and again.
Then I was gone. The sea under your bed said something
like your name: you thought you'd drown.

This morning your fever slinks away
like a dog bested by the hubbub of city-fed
and workaday birdsong come into its own.
You call. You want some toast.

The trees are bone dry; sunlight hunkers behind them.
Your hair fronds when I lift your head
as if out of a sea pulling away. I offer you
the lidded cup. You take it and you drink.

Let the worst I ever do to you be die.
Turn your head sideways, dear, so I can watch you sleep.
Let the morning have us, and the afternoon.
I am here, blessed, capable of more.

Away

I babysit by Skype,
breakfast to their lunch,
lunch to their dinner.

I straighten uniforms, ask French,
nag music practice, argue *Friends*,
trim their Bebo access.

I touch their silky faces on my screen.
I am three thousand miles ago,
five hours in the red.

What would it take —
one crossed cyber wire,
a virtual hair's breadth awry —

for these synapsed hours
to bloat to centuries,
for my background

to be rescinded
to a Botticelli blue,
my webcam image

ruffed and pearled,
speaking vintage words
into spindrift?

Or, failing that,
for me to be headlonged
into light years off

to the room of an obsolete laptop
where I Skype and Skype
and no one answers,

where I Google Earth to see
if the world namechecks
this morning

my son's bike in the garden,
my daughter's skirt
on the line?

Bodkin

A word from a dream, or several, spiked on it
like old receipts. Something akin to a clavicle's
bold airs; a measurement of antique land;
a keepsake brooch on a quilted silk bodice;
a firkin, filled to the brink with mead or milk;
a bobbin spinning like a back-road drunken bumpkin;
borrowed, half-baked prophecies in a foreign tongue;
a debunked uncle's thin bloodline; a Balkan
fairy story, all broken bones poked inside out;
a bespoke book blacked in with Indian ink;
a bobolink in a buckeye or a bare-backed oak;
a barren spindle, choked ankle-high with lichen;
a fistful of ball bearings dropped on a *bodhrán*.
Body skin. Kith and kin. Other buckled things.

Wind in Trees

Tonight the wind tries on fancy dress
in the attic rooms of trees,

crinolines and winkle-pickers,
mustachios and swords,

a jewelled fob-watch keeping time
with my shutters' throb and hum.

Silks crinkle precisely at my window
and, at my door, an ivory cane

is summoning my name.
I ask will anything ever change.

First the trees say 'No' to me.
Then the wind says 'Yes'.

Love Songs

Your email shimmers
in my inbox.

Here are your words,
inestimable, smooth
to my fingertip,
as though, by touch,
they could be made
to open a chink more.

~

I would have you lie down
on young heather,
all the years between us
pressed clean like sheets of linen,
and everything that might have been
come round again
as the sea worn
on your wrists.

~

The bruise on my forearm
puts me in mind
of the hole in your sleeve
through which I would,
if so allowed,
sieve every waking hour.

~

The flare of the mobile phone
in my hand
is an outcrop of sunlight

in which we sit
eavesdropping the gossip
of bracken and fern
while I watch your freckles ripen
to the same shade
as my own.

~

What will I do
when I am too old
for such love songs?

An Teach Tuí

Thistledown, fuchsia, flagstone floor:
this noun house

has the wherewithal
to sit out centuries,

squat between bog-water darkness
and rooms turned inside out to summer,

straw-coloured months of childhood
answering each other

like opposite windows in thickset walls
that sunlight will cajole.

Tea roses bluster the half-door.
Rain from eaves footfalls the gravel.

A robin, cocksure of himself,
frittered away all morning in the shrub.

If I knew how to fix in even one language
the noise of his wings in flight

I wouldn't need another word.

(*An Teach Tuí*: The Thatched House)

Pier

Speak to our muscles of a need for joy.
       — W H Auden, 'Sonnets from China' (XVII)

Left at the lodge and park, snout to America.
Strip to togs, a shouldered towel, flip-flop over
the tarmac past the gangplanked rooted barge,
two upended rowboats and trawlers biding time.
Nod to a fisherman propped on a bollard,
exchange the weather, climb the final steps
up to the ridge. And then let fly. Push wide,
tuck up your knees so the blue nets hold you,
wide-open, that extra beat. Gulp cloud;
fling a jet trail round your neck like a feather boa,
toss every bone and sinew to the plunge.
Enter the tide as if it were nothing,
really nothing, to do with you. Kick back.
Release your ankles from its coiled ropes;
slit water, drag it open, catch your breath.
Haul yourself up into August. Do it over,
raucously. Head first. This time, shout.

Purism

The wind orchestrates
its theme of loneliness
and the rain
has too much glitter in it, yes.

They are like words, the wrong ones,
insisting I listen to sense.
But I too am obstinate.

I have white walls,
white curtained windows.
What need have I
of the night's jet-black,
outlandish ornament?

What I am after
is silence
in proportion
to desire,

the way music plumbs
its surfaces
as straight words do
the air between them.

I begin to learn
the simple thing

burning through
to an impulse at once lovely
and given to love

that will not be refused.

Cowslips

Four times I have thrust my writing hand
into a tuft of cowslips:
once, for starters, in the ditches of childhood,
years later, in a book of Dürer prints,
and then in a Washington gallery, for real,
where I found it proved no more vivid, or less,
than what is growing beside me now in a pot
on my patio. To my left, cowslips;
to my right, a print of cowslips
dislodged from clay and context
except for the vellum's wash of earth
that is a kind of framing device as definite
as these straight and straightforward lines.

Drawn, as it were, on both a horizontal
and a vertical scale, an ardour of leaves
pushing east and west, even out to the margin
of brown ink that squares up to the limits of art.
The leaves are decades, centuries,
each with its own delineation
that matters not a whit. The leaves
are how we live every day, how we spread
a green, embroidered cloth over waking hours.

The flowers are emergence, the flare
of dim brilliance by which we mark our time.
The flowers love the world, have reason to:
they are aspirant, barely beautiful, almost soaked
into the background of golden, besmirched air
that is, always, a morning in 1526
stippling the seal of gouache
to interrupt accomplishment
with creases and the finest cracks
that might be said to breathe;
and are yet discernible as slight rebuke

to years lived in between
as if there were no such cowslips
to be given to such light.

I know it now. I have asked the question
of a flower or print I always lacked the guts
to ask of life. I thought it would be cowslips always,
tufts of them seedling all over my time.

And it has been.

I mean, it was.

3

It is late. The night is required to fold itself up
into squares that get smaller and smaller
the more I notice them. I am learning
to pay attention to this narrow, straight-line house
that must have had all its corners by heart before
ever I came to fit my life snug under its eaves.

I could count the balustrade shadows as standing in
for decades, or for owners, in my stead, and know
it is not for me to believe they left nothing behind:
nothing in how a door will open or a door will close,
or a window lean into what the rowan tree has to say.
The banister's way with three hinged centuries
has more heat in it than it needs to have, even on this
July evening when the rooms at the top of the house
vouchsafe another summer day tomorrow.

I am the clean slate. I am off-white walls
and open windows, a garden planted from scratch.
I am floor-length curtains and bookcases,
rooms that listen nicely to each other.
I am door knobs and reading lamps, blue glass
bowls on window sills, family photographs,
corners with silence in them, that sly peace,
a contrivance to which my blue and white hours
and too much clean bedlinen give the lie.

My house of uneven numbers,
of my children's hyphenated lives.
My house of small hours, of voices
a little quieter than they need to be.
Our summer is all in paragraphs,
everything supposedly given to light,
despite the slip in every corner
with a May date written on it

by ghosts who listen to everything,
but cannot make sense of it; who gather
in their arms what light the house holds,
pooling it in doorways so none of us
will ever have to step out into dark;
who fret the dog every now and then and,
to make up for it, ruffle lavender in its pots
so the scent slips in the back door; who play
noughts and crosses in the trellis shadow
and don't care who loses, who wins.

Fate

I do not know what it is in me
that would want to bunker down

in a fairy story that could nutshell
nine hundred years to my two

and would have me speak
with the throat of a bird

or the throat of a reed
by the side of a lake

with nowhere to go.

That would have me exchange
my blue and white bedroom for feathers,

cups of gold for handfuls of sand,
love for thunder and brine.

Except this. I toy with banishment
a second time and a third

but my heart isn't in it.
I already know

that if I have been required to fly
over the history of my house

and see only nettles and scutch
where my children's home should be,

then I will also be woken by bells
with their eight o'clock definite truth

so I may walk in the room
of my own breath

and say we will leave it at that.

'La Route'

— André Derain (1932)

Three bars of shadow on a yellow road,
a sky of Chinese blue.
Though there is only the road
and its sidelong songs
to mark time with you, walk on.
Trees talking shadow talk
will make no mention of you.

With your ashplant and knapsack
you have no notion of rain
or thunder with no rain in it
scarcely worth sheltering from,
even if the village had roofs
and doors to the houses,
music to its two streets.

If you are sorry, as I was,
that you didn't bring bread with you
and something to wash it down
and maybe a fig for afterwards,
don't give it another thought.
This is one of many villages
that turns its open palms up to the sun.

Next along the yellow road
another town will occur to you,
this time approached by a bridge.
You will hear cowbells and church bells
and a donkey whingeing at them.

You will smell loaves rising
and you will quicken your step
until your footprints in the dust

fall upon footprints in the dust
to lead you to a stranger's door.

No one will be surprised to see you
for your own two children
will be waiting there
with a welcome for you
like a jar of wildflowers
and no harm done.

Is It Time?

The children will be waiting for me
with blue-veined arms and all tomorrow
slaked in the whites of their eyes.

They have knowledge, they assure me,
of how rain comes undone
and mornings thicken like milk.

They remember the story of the night
that popped itself inside out
and forgot all of its songs.

'But what happened the moon?'
Picked up, shiny penny, by a woman
with too much air in her pockets,

spent on a word from a barrow seller
and gifted, in turn, to a boy and a girl
who learn what becomes of it.

When All This Is Done, Sure

If I liken you to anything
it will probably have to be

the small boy on the A-train
with a xylophone on his lap.

When the doors close
nothing is left of him

but precise, metallic silence
where his four right notes have been.

Just Exactly That Kind of Day

A summer Saturday pitched
like a mansard roof made of red tiles,
leftover minutes from the week just gone,
squares of music rehearsing a fall
as ticker tape from open windows
any street you care to cross.

In such a come day, go day kind of town,
I wonder what fractional slippage of love
might think itself so obvious as this.

And the wondering is like
when something's lost
and you look everywhere
but it's not to be found
until there it is
right in front of your eyes

and still you keep on looking.

The Front Door

The sky inside my head grows out
of a single cell of blue. One minute
I'm snicking geraniums and, before you know it,
there's larks and curlews and a jet-trail
with no beginning to it unzipping my last thought.

One minute I'm pinning my to-do list,
like a discouraged orchid, to the day;
the next, here in the kitchen,
the night's two plums are bedding down
in their black lacquer bowl.

Between, the day rises to a skim of meaning,
the bright blue door opening into what
I think I know. Everything else is an eye
of daylight through which is streaming,
time and again, what all happens next.

Going Out

for Eve

My daughter, heading out on the town in her glad rags,
laughs a laugh like a floribunda rose pinned in her hair.
She has so much beauty in her, more than this summer
evening, in all its frippery. More, even, than the sound
of her heels the length of the road, her phone voice
dipping into company, the pooled high talk of her
and her friends slipping through the city's open door.

Do me a favour, daughter: sometime, in time, wear for me
a sweetheart neckline, slingback sandals, my good ring
and howsoever many of your necklaces and bracelets.
Walk your walk through ten thousand doorways
so the music of you is one and the same as the music
of starlings and new moons and traffic lights and weirs,
only in a new arrangement arranged by, and for, you.

The Garden as Event

The briars are twined to the fencing post
and the afternoon staked to two kinds of hour,
the narrow, answered by coffee cups
or birdsong run amok,

the other, stretched to the edge of the city
like the skin of a drum on which
someone is keeping time, bald time,
with a persistent heart.

I could drop a question on its surface
and it would bounce, slight answer
to what the skyline asks of the sky;
the branch, of the cherry tree.

In the milk-white kitchen
nothing has changed for an hour
or more: the lettuce is upright
in the window trough

and the cut-glass vase on the table top
has nothing to add to the square of light
slipping off a neighbour's patio door
one street to the back.

Knives whittle patience in the drawer
and fruit in the fruit bowl glosses
a composed version of itself.
The front door holds its breath.

All this happens, is happening
without me, in much the same way

as the cowslips make sense
of their borrowed pot

or winter slumps in the green bin
or shallow leaves fathom
the azalea I earthed
and the rowan I did not.

The Garden in Hindsight

Those black tulips that never put forth
so much as a single bloom,

would they be as close in themselves
this day as the day we upped sticks

to three houses ago, our belongings
in numbered boxes, seven years

as a handful of soil in a page
between me and my winter coat?

Tonight, as the year hoists itself north,
I imagine them still there, winter

by winter, learning to turn embittered
hearts against all possible sky

and every tulip planted since
a righting of the weight of darkness

pressed by my hand to lodge and yield
as to remembered light.

Ghost Poem

Crowded at my window tonight, your ghosts
will have nothing to speak of but love
though the long grass leading to my door
is parted neither by you, leaving,

nor by you, coming here. The same ghosts
keep in with my blood, the way
a small name says itself, over
and over, so one minute is cavernous

compared to the next, and I cannot locate
words enough to tell you your wrist
on my breast had the same two sounds to it.
You are a sky over narrow water

and the ghosts at my window
are a full day until I shed their loss.
I want to tell you all their bone-white,
straight-line prophecies

but the thought of you, this and every night,
is your veins in silverpoint mapped
on my skin, your life on mine
that I made up and lived inside, as real,

and I find I cannot speak of love
or any of its wind-torn ghosts to you
who promised warm sheets and a candle, lit,
but promised me in words.

High Notes

On a train threading the eye of north
it is nothing to begin to collapse
the various silence the city required of me:
to find in the high notes of the brakes
the scarlet lining of a dark coat
or the single lit office on a top floor;
to listen for the shape of a name
through glass at a station stop;
to observe the fields of an afternoon,
the way they chase each other down
in the kind of blue that learned abstraction
moons ago, how they resolve themselves
into a love poem for no one in particular,
written to be open, for the sake of openness,
this night and every budding night inside.

The Landscapes of Vilhelm Hammershøi

Between water reading itself a story
with no people in it

and fields, illegible, and a sky
that promises nothing,

least of all what will happen now,
are the trees

that do not believe in
any version of themselves

not even the one in which
they are apparently everyday trees

and not a sequence of wooden frames
for ordinary leaves.

Author's Note

The past twenty-one years of publishing poems have been a deal less lonely and more enjoyable than they might have been because of the generous support of my family and friends. Thanks are due especially to John McAuliffe, Ian McGuire, Helen O'Leary, Conor O'Callaghan, Peter Fallon and Carol Mavor. I'm very grateful to The Gallery Press for unfailing hospitality over the course of nine titles, including this one. The University of Manchester, Poetry Ireland and the Arts Council/An Comhairle Ealaíon have all provided crucial support in their various ways. Most of all, though, thanks to Tommy and Eve for keeping pace with all of this, and also for keeping life on the boil, enough that the writing of poems is a boon and a pleasure even yet.